D1530127

Elegant Designs for Paper Cutting

Margaret Keilstrup

Dover Publications, Inc.
Mineola, New York

Copyright

Copyright © 1997 by Dover Publications, Inc.
All rights reserved.

Bibliographical Note

Elegant Designs for Paper Cutting, first published in 2003, is a retitled republication of *Lacy Cut-Paper Designs,* originally published by Dover Publications, Inc., in 1997.

International Standard Book Number: 0-486-29512-5

Manufactured in the United States by Courier Corporation
29512506
www.doverpublications.com

Far more than a delightful children's pastime, paper cutting is a very old art form, dating back almost to the invention of paper by the Chinese. In China and most other parts of the Far East, it is still practiced with great skill and is an important symbolic addition to religious holidays, weddings, funerals and other rites. In Germany, cut-paper images are known as *Scherenschnitte,* and are not only used for decorative shelf-edgings and Christmas trimmings, but are often cut into fanciful or solemn borders for birth, baptismal and wedding certificates, and even to record the death of a loved one. Britain, too, has its paper-cutting heritage. One famous "papyrologist" of the eighteenth century interested King George III and Queen Charlotte in her amazingly intricate art, and nearly everyone in early America tried his or her hand at the cutting of silhouette portraits from the profiles of family and friends. In the form of handmade valentines, paper doilies and Christmas snowflakes, the art passed into the nineteenth century, and on into the machine age of mass-produced—and now laser-cut—paper laces.

But no mechanical process can equal the pleasure of unfolding your own hand-snipped valentine or photo-border and seeing the design emerge as you create it.

The patterns that follow are suitable for bookmarks, calling or business cards, notepaper and stationery borders, photo and document frames, and many other gift and personal items.

Materials and Instructions: The originals of the designs in this book were cut with a small pair of nail scissors that has short, curved blades with very sharp points and can penetrate several layers of paper easily. Certain kinds of embroidery scissors also work well, as do those sold specifically for paper crafts. Fine-bladed craft knives are usable (those with swivel blades are best).

Cut out the design of your choice and fold as indicated, making sure the crease is sharp and clean. Some of the designs are single-fold and other double; one is fan-folded, and one is cut flat, without folding at all. Begin to cut away the blackened areas by piercing a single area with the point of your scissors, then insert the blades into the slit you have pierced and cut with short snips, laying the blade with the curve of the design and making longer, smooth cuts whenever possible. **Do not begin** by cutting away all of the outer border or all of the center space in border designs; you will find it much easier if you leave some of this solid area to hold onto as you work and remove the larger areas last. Intricate designs look difficult, but they are only small, individual cuts; simply work your way from one edge to the other, cutting as smoothly as you can on the curves. Wherever space did not allow for the inclusion of the reduced rendering of a design on the same pages as the folding-and-cutting diagram, they are keyed to each other by letters; this also applies when there is more than one diagram per page. (This only occurs on the last four pages of the book.)

If you cut through a bar, don't despair! You can mend it with tape and trim the tape as close to the edge of the mistake as you can. Or you can even leave the mistake alone and glue the two edges down to your backing paper carefully when you're finished. You can even reshape the design around your mistake and create an entirely personal paper cutting all your own! Paper is an amazingly flexible and adaptable medium, and you might like to add to the beauty of your designs with colored pencil or watercolors, touch them with gilt paper, or weave narrow ribbon into the borders.

Many kinds of glue can be purchased for mounting. I prefer a spray adhesive, used lightly so as not to soak through the paper. (Spray the back of the cutting itself, not the mounting paper, or you will have sticky spots where the backing shows through!) Glue sticks are fine, but drier types such as removable stick-on glues for memos, etc., are less likely to tear the finely cut paper.

For backing your finished designs, choose heavier paper such as construction paper. I prefer watercolor and other artists' papers, which come in a wide range of colors and give a firm, stable backing that is unlikely to fade or bleed into the cutting as construction paper may do in time.

Good luck, and enjoy exploring the art of hand-cut paper lace!

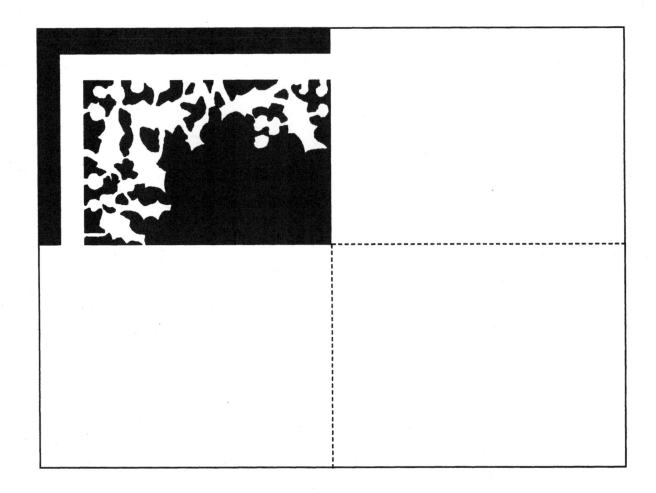

3

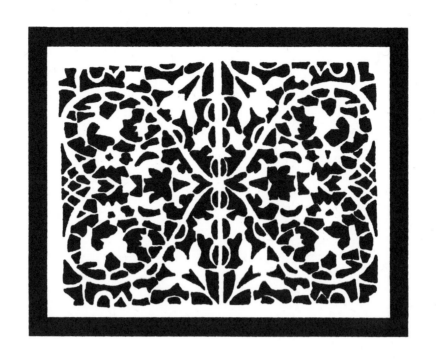

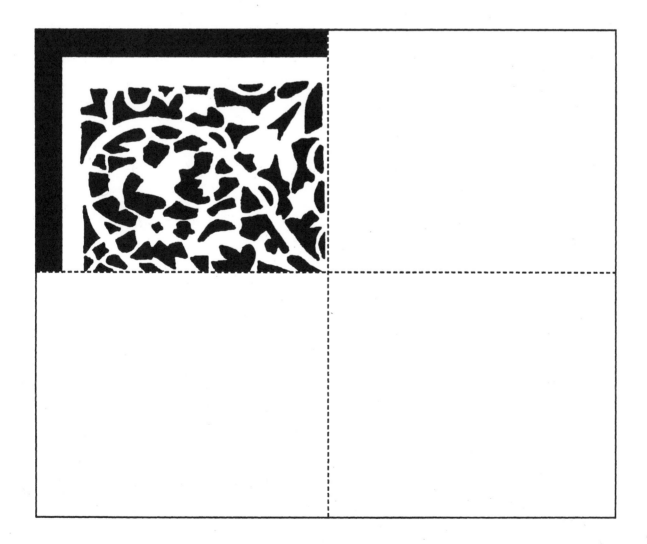

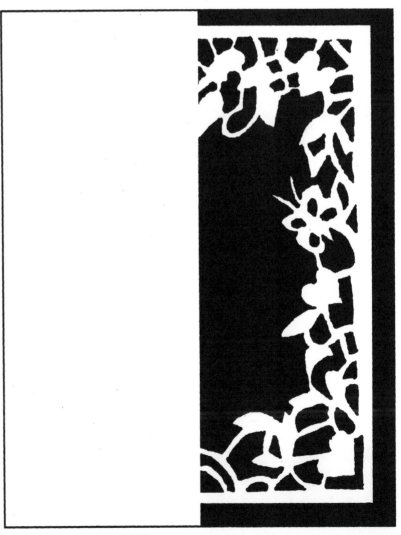

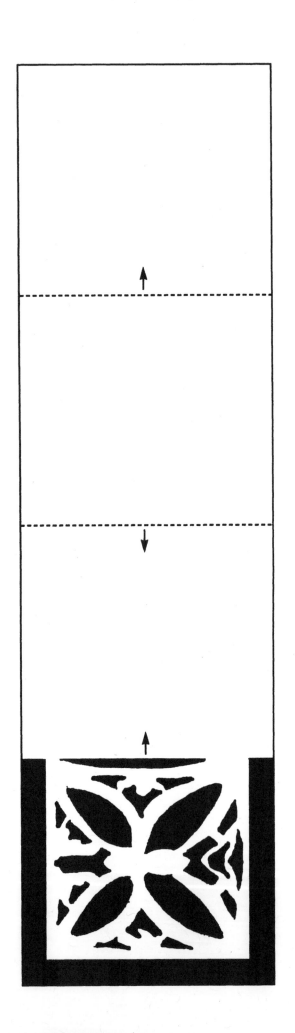

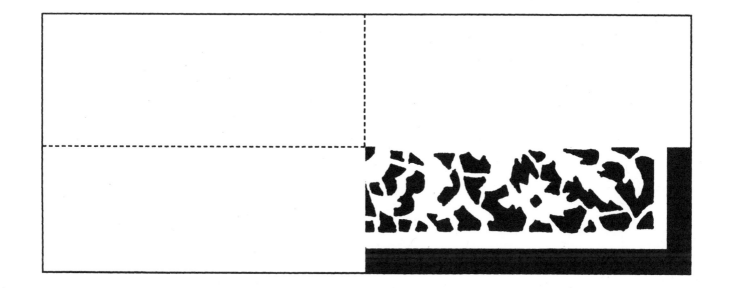

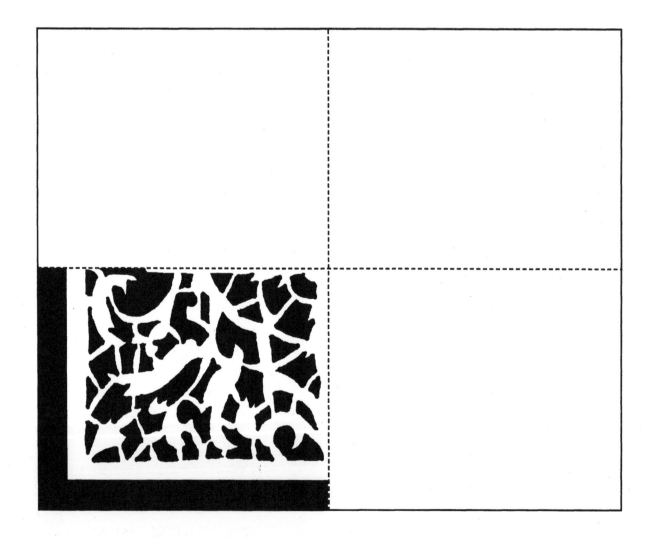

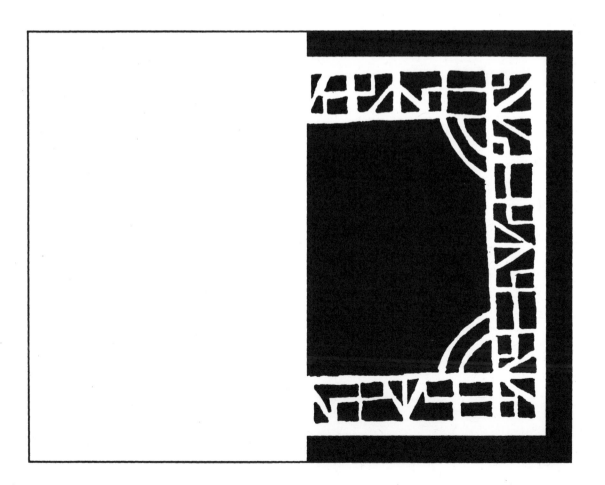

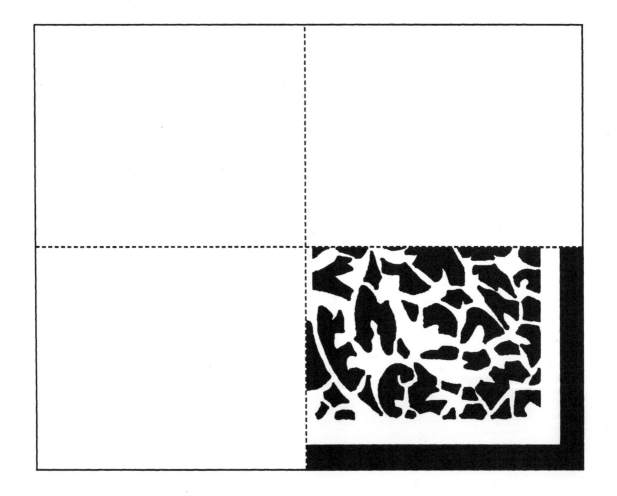

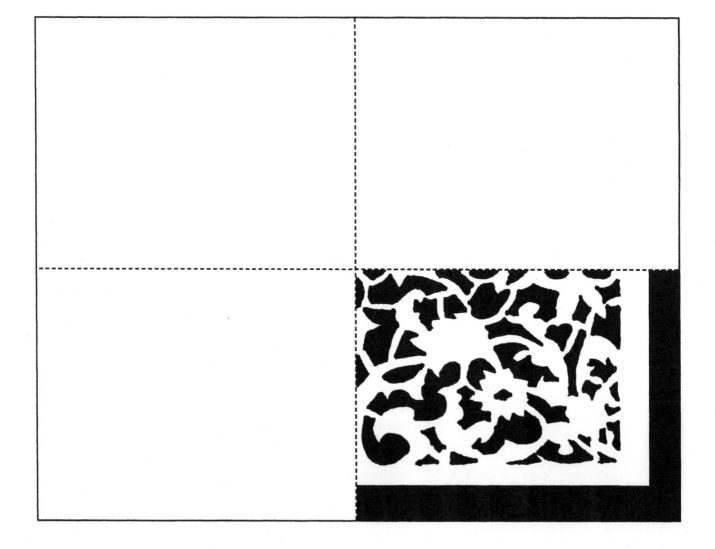

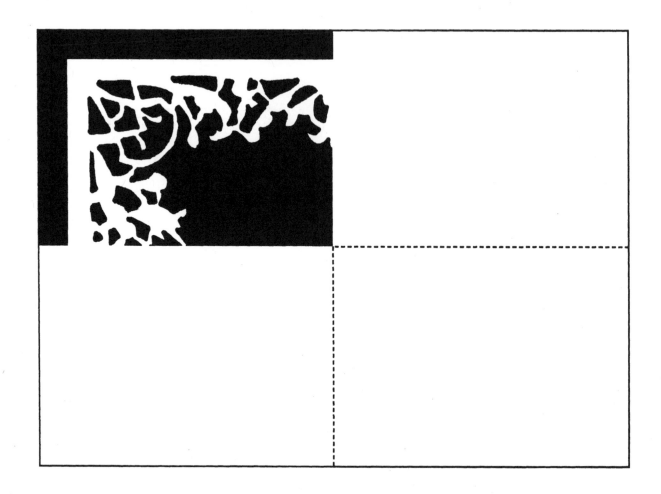

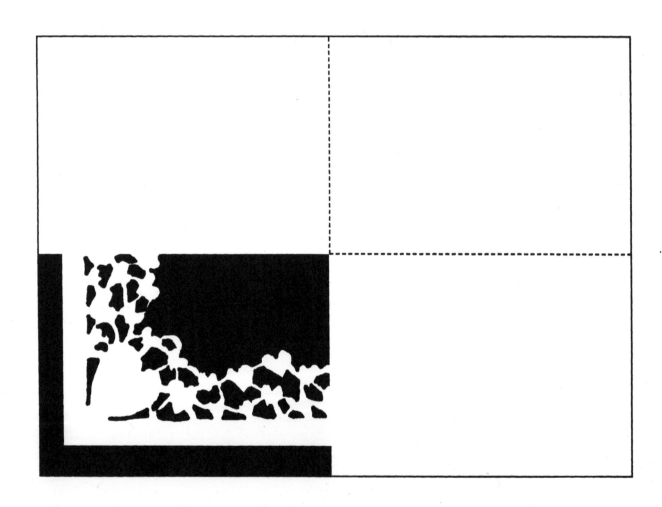

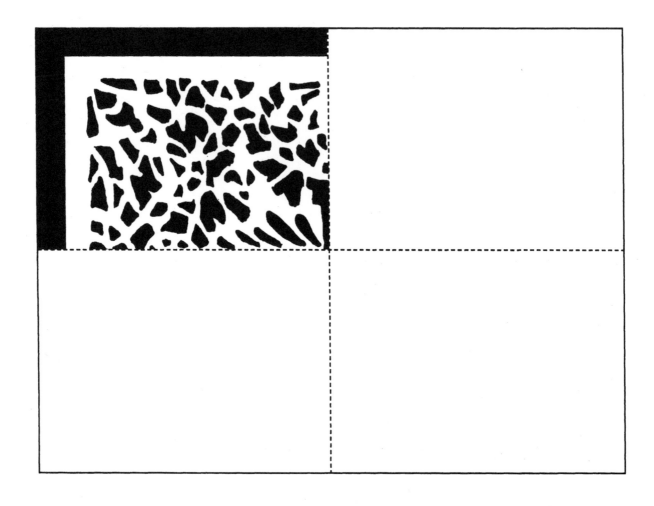

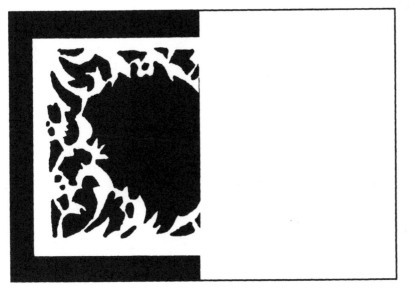

A

A

B

B

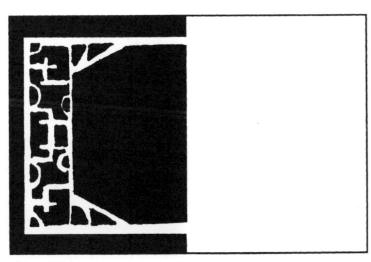

C

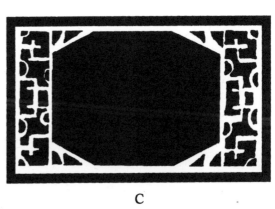

C

29

D

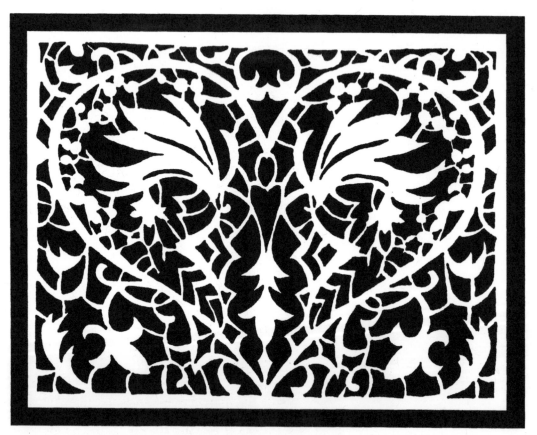E

D

E